Transitions Operation DD214 and Beyond

Melody Young

Published by Melody Young, 2022.

TRANSITIONS OPERATION DD214 AND BEYOND

First edition. December 20, 2022.

ISBN: 979-8215819975

Written by Melody Young.

Table of Contents

This guide is dedicated to the many servicemen and women who have left or are contemplating completely leaving military service for civilian life.

As a Veteran, I am grateful for my loving and supportive Family and the other Veterans who helped guide me along the way in this new way of life.

I praise God for giving me His Love, Strength and Hope that saw me through the dark days and helped lift me up to a better place, mentally, emotionally and spiritually.

TRANSITIONS

OPERATION "DD214"...and Beyond

Introduction

We have all heard the military term "Operation" such as in "Operation Enduring Freedom". It usually represents a major military campaign that involves multiple branches in various locations around the world.

For the purposes of this guide, the term "Operation DD214" represents the major endeavor that servicemen and women undertake when they start on the path towards civilian life. Complete civilian life, not as a reservist or guard member, but a complete and total severing of military service. This "operation" can be lengthy, tiring, and at times frustrating.

Transitions will guide you step by step on your transition out of military service back into life as a full time civilian. I know your thinking "but I have the perfect plan and I'll make sure to complete the transition assistance program the military gives me". Well that's all well and good, but those classes and programs are all to help with your plan **A**. This guide reinforces that plan from a different perspective and helps you develop plans for if Plan A falls apart or is not what you really wanted or expected.

What was the inspiration for this guidebook? Prior to my discharge, I, like many of you, thought I had the perfect plan in place. I was going back to school and afterwards going to start a brand new career. I had a nice savings and would use my post 9/11 benefits to not only pay for school but assist in my housing payments until complete.

Well the school part happened, but only after a few unexpected changes with not only the school, but the program I wanted to pursue and the city I would be living in. In the midst of the turmoil, my savings were wiped out, My family became temporarily homeless, and I broke my wrist, all within the first two years after leaving the service. I use the first person, but in reality everything affects not only you but your entire immediate family, especially if you are a head of household.

I have gone through every plan that will be discussed in this guide. I will tell you both how to succeed in whatever situation or plan you are in, and how to avoid some of the pitfalls and mistakes I made and many people make when transitioning out of the military.

This guide stems from those learned experiences, dealing with school, work, relocation and oh the much dreaded Veterans Administration system. My life is not perfect now, but I've become an entrepreneur, an author and have a beautiful home.

Let's begin by evaluating where you are at this point in your military career and why you are leaving the service. Are you retiring? If not, have you accomplished all that you desired with your military career or are you just tired of it all and looking for a new start? How are your finances? Do you have another job lined up? Do you have savings for at least 12 months of expenses?

The answers to these questions will determine a lot of what direction you should be looking into and what level of planning needs to happen prior to discharge. If your discharge is involuntary make sure you have exhausted all of your options to appeal, including your chain of command, chaplain, mental health counseling, and if necessary, judge advocate counseling.

The following assessment will help in developing your Plan A. It may be that unless you're retiring, discharging may not be the best option at this time. So let's get started.

Transitions..."Operation DD214"

Where are you now?

Self Evaluation

As mentioned in the introduction, let's do a quick review of where you are now.

Answer the following questions:

Are you retiring? **YES** or **NO**

If **YES** when?

If you are within 6 months of retirement, continue to build on savings, confirm or establish. health care for you and your family. Make sure you have a minimum of 12 months living expenses saved to start your retirement, preferably in high interest earning accounts and/or in diversified funds such as IRA's, stocks, bonds, etc.

If you are outside of 6 months, and have not yet started to grow your savings, now is the time to get that process started. Speak to a financial advisor regarding what products would maximize your investments and potential for return..

Now is also the time to think about what you may want to do employment wise. Do you want to take an extended vacation? Travel? Start a business? Or start a new career. Take advantage of your remaining months to research what you will need in order to not have to work, work part time and have enough for everyday and unexpected expenses for you and your household.

If your answer is **NO**, then answer the following:

When is your discharge date?

If your discharge date is within 6 months, you should have already saved a minimum of 6 months of living expenses at double whatever your current monthly living expenses are. So for example, if your monthly expenses, including utilities, are around $2,000.00, you should have approximately 4,000 a month for 6 months saved up, that's $24,000.00 at a minimum. Or, 12 months of savings at $2,000.00 a month also totalling $24,000.00 in savings.

Savings can and should be a combination of traditional banking, and investment products such as stocks, bonds, and mutual funds. In other words, it should be diversified. In addition, at least 50% should be easily liquidated meaning it can be quickly turned into cash.

If your discharge is outside of 6 months, and you don't have a sizable savings, consider if you really want to discharge at this time. Especially if, just a few more years say, 5 or under will put you at retirement.

Achieving your plan A will be much easier if you have retired and have those additional benefits that come with retirement, along with lifetime healthcare, which in and of itself is priceless.

If you have more than 5 years remaining and/or are just tired of military life and all of the challenges that come with it, then your discharge time frame becomes even more critical as you have a lot more work to do.

Ask yourself, can your household fully function without your current income for 6 months or more?

If the answer is **YES**, good, you and your family have a safety net that doesn't include you, which will be needed if your Plan A fails and you don't have that 24k in savings.

If the answer is **NO**, and you are **within** 6 months of non-retirement discharge, reconsider discharging at this time, or at the very least consider reenlisting into the Reserves or National Guard and have a job lined up with a start date immediately upon your discharge.

If the answer is **NO**, and you are **outside** 6 months of discharge, look into postponing or pushing back that date if possible to give yourself time to make some financial adjustments. In the meantime take or request any extra or additional duty assignments you can get to plus up your savings.

For all answers, make sure you have completed any training and doctor's appointments so there is no delay with starting your VA benefits. If you will be returning to school, make sure your enrollment paperwork and processes are completed and any housing arrangements settled.

Plan A

What are your post military goals?

What are the steps you need to take to realize your dream, everything you hope to accomplish or achieve after life in the service? Whether it be an advanced degree, expanding your family, becoming a business owner or buying or building that dream home.

Plan A is what you start building on now, before your discharge has been finalized and you have been set free back into civilian life.

What is your desire after discharge regarding.....

a. Work/Career
b. School or Continuing Education
c. Travel or Vacation

Work or Career

If you plan on going right into another job or career field have you researched the qualifications and any additional education or certifications you might need? If you're within 6 months of discharge have you started putting in job applications?

Many people want to go directly from service to traditional employment with only a small break for relocation and or family vacation. In this case, you should already have your offer letter with a starting date in hand.

Higher Education or Certification?

If you are going back to school in order to acquire knowledge, skills and or certification for a specific job or career field make sure the career field is definitely what you want to do before committing to an educational program. Your education benefits are not unlimited, plus going back to school as an adult can be emotionally, and physically taxing.

I found this out the hard way. I picked a profession that sounded interesting and thought it would be a good fit for me but after changing schools and entering the course, I found out that it wasn't what I really wanted to invest my time and energy into, and the financial payoff wasn't what I thought it was going to be either.

From there, I jumped right into another program that sounded good and spent the next 2 years struggling to complete a program and work in a career field I thought I would enjoy and did for a time, only to lose it as soon as the coronavirus pandemic caused a lot of medical services to be scaled back. Being a new graduate, it was difficult for me to find employment against other more qualified candidates.

The lesson, don't rush into an educational program, until you've had a chance to do more research on the career field, both pros and cons. This includes meeting and talking to people who work in the profession to determine if it is indeed what you want to do. Unlike a job that you can change, you can't get your educational benefits back, nor the time, and hard work you put into that program should you realize this isn't the right fit.

Once you've made a decision, go ahead and submit your application to your desired school. I recommend an in person or hybrid program if you're going back to school for the first time in quite a few years. You want to make sure you have been accepted and know what your course path will be. Next, verify the cost of the program will be fully covered by your education benefits. If not, what will the uncovered costs be and how will they be paid.

Finally, make sure you understand how long your acceptance is good for and are there any prerequisites you will be required to take. Perhaps you can take some courses (one or two) online prior to your full discharge.

Travel or Vacation - Let's take a trip.

Most people will want to take some time off before starting a new job or going back to school. Do it, you and your family deserve it for all your years of service and sacrifice. Go someplace where you will get plenty of fun and relaxation, but don't forget to do your research.

If you are going overseas, make sure you register with the appropriate federal agencies for travel safety. Oftentimes the State Department will issue do not travel, or travel with caution alerts for certain countries.

These are important because it means your safety has a higher chance of being threatened due to internal conflicts going on within that country or region or high rates of crimes against tourists.

In addition, as part of your research, include reviews and cancellation policies for hotel and travel arrangements. Only use reputable and verified resources. Double and triple check hotel and travel arrangements . Safety is everything.

If remaining stateside, still double check all of your arrangements, make sure you understand any cancellation policies in case you need to make a last minute change in travel plans.

Housing - where will you live?

This actually is the first decision you will make. Are you planning on relocating back to your home of record? Or perhaps you love the city and state where you are? This decision will influence your budget, career field and school choices.

Although the government will move your household goods after your discharge to your desired location, traveling and moving your family can be quite expensive. You don't get extra funds to set up your new home. Those expenses come out of pocket and should be added to your financial planning if you plan on relocating to another state.

Second, finding housing will take time. If possible, plan a visit to the state and city you're interested in. Include cost of living, and housing in various neighborhoods.

If you have children, look at school ratings. Make sure they include test scores and graduation rates. Last but not least, employment outlook and options.

Consider areas close to a military installation. This gives you access to many programs, assistance and activities in a familiar environment. Many bases also offer additional counseling and transition assistance for newly separated veterans. Shopping at the commissary will also be a big savings for you and your family.

If you are relocating back to your home of record, go back and visit to see what changes may have taken place. Check out the areas you are interested in moving back to and see if the cost of living and housing costs have changed.

Financial Planning

Once you have made a decision regarding housing, complete development of your financial plan. This plan should include not only enough for relocation expenses, but enough money for food, housing, utilities and vehicle maintenance for 12 months. That's right, one whole year.

When you are within 6 months of discharge you will probably begin your transition planning courses which include, developing a financial plan and budget. This will look good on paper, but the reality will be different. My suggestion: find a house or apartment complex near where your desired location is and find out how much on average the monthly rent or mortgage is, then multiply that by 12. Then take that number and cut it in half, that will be your food and utilities, now add that back to your housing costs. You get the point. In addition, you should have at least $5,000.00 put to the side for unexpected car or house repairs.

These figures may seem high, but there's no guarantee you will get that dream job, or complete or even start school. Paying bills outside of the military is a whole lot different than when you're in, with a housing, food and clothing allowance.

Recommended Financial Plan:

12 months or more remaining:

- Start saving with a Thrift Savings Plan - this tax free plan is a good funds matching plan that will help you save more, quicker.

- Consider investing in a diversified stock program (stocks, mutual funds, real estate) - there are quite a few to choose from, look into those with minimum to moderate risk. Consider meeting with a financial counselor.

- Re-evaluate your savings accounts, are you earning the best interest rate? Don't be afraid to consider other banks which may offer better rates.

- Start working on your credit score, make sure you are paying bills on time and catching up on any delinquencies making them current. Try to clear as many high interest rates debts you have first.

6 months or less remaining:

- Make sure your budget planning matches your calculations for required savings. If they don't you will need to increase your investment deposits or reconsider your discharge timing, if that is an option.

- Find out how long you can keep your Thrift Savings Plan before you need to withdraw or transfer the funds.

- Make sure you have full accountability for your supply turn-ins. If you have any charges, either dispute them or plan to have them paid prior to discharge. You don't want to have any unexpected deductions from your remaining DFAS checks or expected IRS refunds.

Healthcare

If you are retiring make sure you and eligible family members are registered with Tricare as you will have access to military hospitals and any facility that accepts TriCare. You will be eligible for TriCare for life once you reach age 65 and have signed up for Medicare parts A and B.

If you are just doing an expiration of service discharge, then research what your healthcare options are. You may still be eligible for TriCare at least for a certain time. Take the time to sign up with the Veterans Administration (VA) and make sure they have all of your medical paperwork, to make sure you get the highest percentage if you qualify for a disability rating. Now is the time to get those appointments done for any and everything healthcare related for you and your dependents.

There are also many other benefits to registering with the Veterans Administration, some of which include counseling services and eligibility for home purchase assistance with a VA loan. Many cities have local area veteran (VET) centers which will help make this process easier.

This covers most if not all of the primary factors to consider for your plan A. If you take the time to do your research, do some groundwork such as visiting areas of potential relocation and build up your savings, you will be in a good position on your way out the door.

Assignment

For each of the above categories, complete the required information. For example, for the healthcare section, make a list of what the enrollment options are for you and your family and related costs. Include requirements, and any enrollment cutoff dates.

THE DD214

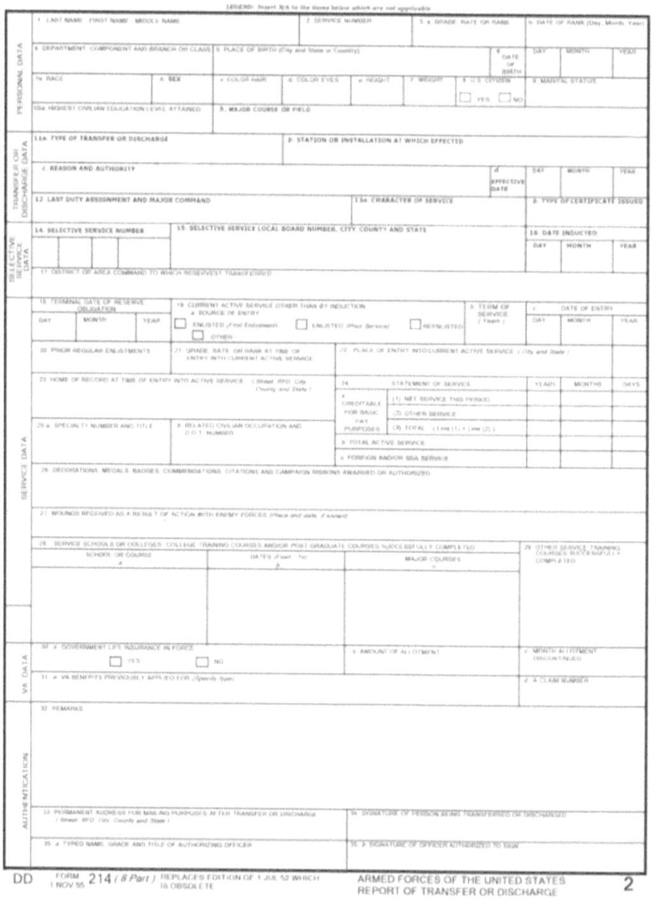

DD FORM 1 NOV 55 214 (8 Part) REPLACES EDITION OF 1 JUL 52 WHICH IS OBSOLETE ARMED FORCES OF THE UNITED STATES REPORT OF TRANSFER OR DISCHARGE 2

A key component of your transition out of the military is receiving the famous or infamous (depending on how you view it) **DD214**. It is the one document that represents the finality of your military career and all you've accomplished.

Some people have multiple DD214's, such as those that have discharged and reenlisted more than once or changed service branches. The importance of this document cannot be overstated. You will receive a draft of your DD214 to approve before it is officially signed off on and released to you and your permanent record. It is critically important to take the time to make sure it is thorough and correct, so let's take a moment to briefly discuss what you should make sure it reflects.

First, make sure all your **personal information** is correct, including spelling of your entire name.

Second, verify all the **dates** they have listed for your enlistment and active duty time. This is important because it is what determines and establishes your retirement years and points.

Third, **awards and medals**, make sure they are all there, even if this means combing through your many years of personal military documents. Keep in mind, Certificates of Achievement and Appreciation normally won't be on there.

Fourth, **campaigns**, make sure every campaign and "operation" you were a part of is included. Any of your assignments within a war zone or hostile environment make you a combat veteran.

Fifth, **type of discharge**, it should be honorable, if it is other than honorable, investigate why and if there is anything that can be done to have it changed to honorable. If it is dishonorable, it will greatly affect how you are seen when it comes to many opportunities such as employment. It may also affect what benefits you are eligible for, so seek counseling including with JAG (Judge Advocate General) if necessary, to appeal a negative discharge.

Last but not least, your **RE code**. RE stands for reenlistment eligibility and it lets recruiters know if you are eligible for reenlistment: make sure it is a 1. Any other number represents something pertaining to the reasons for your discharge and may make you ineligible to reenlist or only under certain conditions. If this is a mistake, have it fixed right away, if it is not, inquire with your transition counselor or Human Resources Sergeant or Officer to see if there is anything that can be done to change the status of your discharge. This will be important if you want to have reenlistment as an option in the future.

So in review, verify the accuracy of these items on your DD214:

Personal information, Enlistment and Active duty dates, Awards and Medals, Campaigns and Operations, Discharge Type, and RE code.

The Veterans Administration

Unless you are retiring you should begin your registration with the Veterans Administration (VA) prior to your discharge. Those receiving a medical discharge or who are being chaptered out may go through a different process.

For most, this will be a formal appointment with a VA representative to go over everything in your medical records. This is very important because if there are any gaps in treatment or not properly documented injuries or illnesses it can affect your disability rating if you are eligible for one.

When you go for your final medical exam make sure you mention every medical issue you are experiencing or have experienced during your time in service.

Not every medical issue will be eligible for a rating but have it documented anyway because if the condition worsens overtime, you will have it documented that it existed prior to discharge which will be critical to the VA compensation and disability review board when it comes to determining an increase in rating.

You should also have your dependent's, including spouse's information, put into the system because that will also affect what type and the amount of benefits you may be eligible to receive.

Meeting with your local VA representative prior to discharge, will alleviate some of the frustrations and delay many veterans face post discharge. After your discharge is complete you will take your coveted DD214 either to your local Veterans Center or closest VA hospital to get your Veterans Identification card. This card gives you access to military installations upon completion of a background check, that is done annually.

If you have not completed the disability rating process or if you have, and you were not given a rating your card will just be your picture, expiration date, identification number and barcode. If you have a rating 10% or above that is service connected make sure the words "service connected"are stated on your card.

A service connected VA card allows you to shop at both post exchanges and commissaries due to a law passed a few years ago that allows veterans with service connected disabilities to shop on bases with just their Veterans ID.

This ID will also be used when you are checking in for appointments at any VA hospital or clinic or if you are shopping or dining somewhere that offers veterans discounts and want proof of service.

The first half of "Operation DD214 " is now complete, now it's time for the rest which in some cases will be even more challenging.

Situation B - What Happened

So you've crossed that big line and become a full time civilian again but your plan **A**, has hit a few snags or bumps. Here are a few possible curbs to your great plan.

Work / Career

You didn't land that dream job because...

a. There were no openings in your area
b. You were unable to acquire the proper credentials
c. They wanted more experience

OR

You landed the dream job but didn't keep it because...

a. You realize that type of job isn't suitable for you
b. The job was highly stressful
c. It pays much less than you thought it would
d. The commute was too long

School

You weren't accepted to your school of choice because...

a. High school or college GPA not high enough
b. Missing required documents
c. Other test scores, ACT, SAT, GRE, GMAT scores not high enough

OR

You were accepted to your school of choice but didn't continue because...

a. Commute was too far
b. Additional costs were unexpected
c. You hated the program you were enrolled into
d. Struggled with studies or other required coursework

Housing

You weren't able to live in the home or area you desired because...

a. Home prices or rent rates were higher than expected
b. Not many suitable apartments or homes available
c. You didn't meet the income threshold
d. Poor or low credit score

OR

You were able to move into your desired home or apartment but moved because..

a. Monthly payments were higher than planned
b. Utilities were higher than planned or expected

c. Undesirable neighbors or neighborhood
d. Cost of living higher than planned
e. Increase in crime
f. Public school ratings low

Finances

Three months after discharge, still financially stable but...

• All remaining pay has been received including any remaining vacation pay

• VA disability rating not confirmed yet or payments not started

• Monthly expenses are financially starting to strain funds

• Must decide whether to find lower income employment or wait for better opportunity regarding Plan A

Six months after discharge, financial stability weakened

• Started dipping into savings to pay monthly bills or cover unexpected expenses such as car repair.

• Temporarily decided to postpone returning to school

- Decided to look for lower paying job with lower qualifications for hire

- May have to relocate to cheaper housing or area with lower cost of living

- Disability rating is low or payments don't cover much in household expenses

Twelve months after discharge, no longer financially stable.

- Savings continue to be drained, there may be less than half remaining

- Lower income work is barely enough to cover monthly expenses

- Starting to reconsider if school is a viable option to increase options

- Mental strain or emotional stress may be more frequent

- Heavily reliant on tax refund

- Any unexpected expense may drain remaining savings

Plan B

Do I make small or big changes?

The good news is in situation B you are still in a good place to get things back on track at 3 months and 6 months after discharge. However, at 12 months, things become a little more difficult. So let's look into options at 6 and 12 months for Plan B.

6 month options

- ➢ Meet with a social services representative from the Veterans Administration to make sure all eligible benefits are being accessed

- ➢ Meet with soldier for life or other branch veteran service agency to see what service or employment assistance you may be able to receive

- ➢ Scale back on any unnecessary purchases or monthly expenses.

- ➢ Restrain from using savings to pay for expenses unless absolutely necessary

- ➢ Consider meeting with a resume coach to develop a more thorough experience driven resume. There are courses that specialize on how to craft your resume for specific jobs.

➢ Look into government jobs that will allow transfer of military time to go towards retirement on the civil service side.

➢ If you are an entrepreneur make sure you are applying for any financial assistance and grants you are eligible for, to help your business get through its first year, which can be the most difficult and costly.

➢ If you are returning to school make sure you have researched the cost, requirements and time for completion. If you are using your post 9/11 or other educational benefits such as the Montgomery G.I. Bill, make sure you are in a program that you definitely want to pursue as a career because once those benefits are used up, they're gone forever.

---

12 month options

➢ If plan B employment isn't sufficient, consider your reenlistment options. Meet with a recruiter to see if you can be brought back in and placed with a unit without going back through MEPS (Military Entrance Processing Station).

I recommend reserves or national guard so you can continue to pursue other goals on the civilian side. This will give you additional income to help with small bills, tuition assistance, insurance, access to commissary and the option to get put on orders should you need additional finances.

➢ Look into temporary federal and private contracting assignments, some are overseas, but most pay really well and will give you and your family a financial boost and perhaps additional training you can use to add to your skillset.

➢ Now may also be the time to look into gig work. Also known as a side job, or side hustle. This type of work is something you can do in your spare time such as UBER or DoorDash food and grocery delivery.

If you have a talent or skill such as photography, web design or cooking, look into getting licensed and insured so you can book clients and events for extra income.

Assignment

Establish your plan B using the 6 month and 12 month options mentioned previously. For example:

6 months from discharge:

★ What is the name and contact information for my VA and or recently separated servicemember representative?

- List here (include, phone, address and email information)

★ Have I updated my resume to include recent training or new skills?

- **YES** or **NO**

★ Have I created a profile and built a resume on USAJOBS to search and apply for federal employment that will allow transfer of military time?

(part of your outprocessing classes is resume building)

- **YES** or **NO**

★ What expenses can me and my family scale back on or eliminate?

12 months from discharge:

If current income isn't sufficient. Have I looked into temporary assignments, part time work or supplemental "gig" work? If yes, which ones am I signed up with?

- List 3 jobs I can do with little or no experience

- List 3 jobs I will do for less pay with or without training

Situation C - What's going on

Situation C is where you have a toe grip on Situation B and your other foot is close to stepping on a banana peel facing towards Situation D. In this stage, your savings are either gone or soon will be, your gig job is probably now your primary job or equal with your main job.

This is also the stage where you reevaluate whether you want to try to continue to achieve your original goals in plan A or go in a completely different direction.

Your situation C normally begins once you have passed 12 months from discharge and have lost your financial cushion. For good or bad, this situation is usually brief and the decisions made during this situation will either help you regain financial stability or you slip entirely into situation D.

Plan C

What to do now

You never actually think you'll need a plan C so it will be hard to develop one with conflicting emotions regarding your current state. That being said, life happens and if you are a former service member you know one thing they train you in the service is adapting to overcome and maintaining situational awareness.

The goal and purpose of this plan is to help get you back solidly into situation or state B. You will primarily be working lower wage jobs, including some form of part time or "gig" work such as delivery driver.

Your income will be almost exclusively going towards food, housing, utilities and any necessary childcare expenses. However, with the proper counseling and guidance you should be utilizing any additional training opportunities to obtain better employment and rebuild your savings.

It can be disheartening working for a check that's barely enough to pay bills let alone save, however, it is crucial that you continue to put in the extra effort to get back on sound footing.

Continue to apply for federal jobs through various federal employment websites. Those jobs are extremely competitive so you may need to apply for a job on a lower skill or pay level to get your foot in the door. Many federal jobs will enable you to buy your military time back towards retirement.

If you have a computer, or access to one, such as the public libraries, consider taking online courses to increase skills or certification. Also, consider paid training programs or programs that will offer you tuition assistance and employment upon completion, such as Nursing.

When you have built back up some of your savings, (I recommend at least 3 months of living expenses), consider making a small investment into something that will bring you a future return on investment such as stocks, bonds or real estate.

Assignment

List the steps you are taking to move back towards situation B for the following:

Savings

→ **Are you able to save?**

- If so, how much?

- If not, how can that be changed?

Work/Career

→ **What type of job(s) are you working?**

- Are they paying a sustainable wage?

- Would you consider making it a career?

- If so, what steps do you need to take?

- If not, what other plans do you have?

→ **Are you in training for another profession?**

→ Are you steadily applying for other jobs?

Housing and Family

→ Are your monthly rent/mortgage payments affordable?

- If not, what actions are you taking?

- Refinancing?

- Additional employment?

- Looking for more affordable housing?

→ Is your family settled?

- Children in school?

- Spouse has stable income?

- Are there any health issues?

Veterans Assistance- Have you met with an advisor for:

- Counseling?

- Financial Assistance?

- Housing Assistance?

- Other eligible benefits including education?

Situation D - What's Happening

In this situation, all of your previous plans have failed, or fallen by the wayside, either temporarily or permanently, and you are quickly slipping out of plan C.

Unemployment or lack of sufficient income can quickly lead to homelessness or inadequate housing which will lead to feelings of what I call, the three D's, **Denial**, **Despair** and finally **Depression**. Situation D is the hardest state, not just because of loss of income or stability but because of the toll it takes on one's mental health.

Things look hopeless and you struggle with what you have done with your life and how things could have turned out this way after all your hard work.

Assignment

Evaluate where you are. What is the state of your physical, financial, and mental health?

Remember your first evaluation took place before your discharge. Now that cord has been cut, and you are in a completely different place from where you imagined you would be at this point in time. Your answers to these questions will determine if you are able to sustain yourself and your family with your current income.

If you are falling behind on payments or are struggling to make payments on time, along with other expenses such as food, you are on a slippery slope towards or perhaps may be in the beginning stages of situation **D**.

> ➢ **Physically** - where are you living? Do you have housing for you and your family? Are you in a safe environment? Do you have transportation or access to public transportation? Having a safe place to lay your head and bathe is critical. Most jobs require you to have an address, including schools if you have young children.
>
> If you don't have stable housing and consider yourself homeless, see what shelters allow you to use their

address as a place of residence. If you have relatives you can stay with temporarily, perhaps they would also be willing to allow you to use their address.

Offer or negotiate some portion of your income no matter how small, as a contribution towards household expenses. There is a more detailed section on the state of homelessness later in this guide.

Maintaining your health is also very important in this situation. Make sure you are keeping your VA appointments and taking any prescribed medication. If you become sick, don't be afraid to take a day or two to get any required treatment and rest.

➢ **Financially** - Are your savings entirely gone? If so, all of your income will be going entirely towards food and housing, there is nothing left for extras, such as fast food or new clothes.

Make sure you have applied for any assistance you are eligible for. There is now a program with the Veterans Administration where they assist you with finding housing and potentially financial assistance to help with food and other expenses.

If you didn't already start in your plan C, now is the time to start that second job. No matter what the income. If you have a reliable car, consider becoming a delivery driver. I recommend work only in areas that won't cause you to drive far, to, from and in between deliveries.

Compare delivery services for base pay, and driver support. Driving for hours, long distances, for low base pay and little or no tip, will be a waste of time and unneeded wear and tear on your vehicle.

If you weren't considering it before, talk to a recruiter, you may still be able to reenlist. It may not be your desire, but there may be opportunities to get a reenlistment bonus for certain specialties.

At this point, your main goal is financial stability and if that means reenlisting, even if you have to go back through basic training, at least you will still be getting paid. Perhaps you will be able to go to school for a MOS in demand that will also give you better career options for life outside the military.

- **Mentally** - Being in an unstable financial situation where you have lost everything you've spent years working hard to accumulate can be devastating emotionally, and depressing mentally.

  Your mental health during this time is extremely critical to overcoming this unexpected setback. If possible seek counseling.

  Most VA clinics and hospitals offer mental health counseling services. If you are a part of a church or religious organization, see who you can talk to who is empathetic but can also offer viable solutions.

  In addition, take advantage of opportunities to rest, relax or even have a moment of fun. That includes walks in the park, if you're close to a beach, having a beach day, watching an old movie or even playing a board game with friends and family. These moments may be brief and few and far between but they are necessary.

  It's ok to take a moment to grieve a failed plan, but don't wallow in sorrow over it. Be sad, then shake the dust off and keep moving forward.

Plan D
Determination

In actuality, plan D doesn't start off as a plan at all, as you never imagine yourself ever having to create one or be in that situation. I call this plan the fourth "D" , the **determination** plan. The climbing your way out of the hole plan. Everything you do in this plan will be not only for survival but your way of saying your life's not over and you can still have a better, more prosperous life.

Having to make a plan D is not the end of the world, and it does not make you a horrible person, parent or veteran. Life happens, sometimes things happen that are out of our control such as sickness, car failures, layoffs etc. where even the best plans aren't enough. It is in those times that we put our training into effect.

Adjust, Adapt and Overcome with faith, perseverance and determination.

Assignment

Developing your plan D Start developing this plan while you are in situation C

If you lost everything in the next 6 months what would you do? Go through each section listed: Housing, Finances, Transportation, etc. and answer the questions.

List the questions and answers in a notebook or in the back of this guide, so you can refer to them later. Keep this updated as changes occur.

I. What is your financial situation?

➢ Where do you work? What is your salary or rate of pay, and how often are you paid, such as hourly, or bi- weekly? Also, does this job offer benefits such as healthcare (medical, dental), 401K etc.?

➢ Do you have any savings or investments remaining, and if so, how much?

➢ Do you have any additional income? If so, from what source(s) and how much are you receiving each month?

➢ Besides housing and utilities, what and how much are your additional monthly expenses? Include everything from credit cards and insurance payments to subscriptions.

2. What is your transportation situation?

➢ If you have a car do you have a note? If so, how much?

➢ What are you spending on gas monthly?

3. Do you have children? If so, how many?

➢ What are their monthly expenses?(include childcare)

4. Health

➢ Do you have healthcare for yourself and your children?

➢ Are there any health issues that require monthly prescriptions?

➢ What, if any, are your out of pocket healthcare expenses?

5. Housing

➢ House or Apartment

○ Including Utilities, what is your monthly payment?

○ Do you own your home? If so, will you be able to continue the mortgage payments with loss of primary income?

○ If you have a lease, when does it end and will you be able to continue making payments with loss of primary income?

➢ Staying with Family or Friend

○ Are you contributing to the household expenses? If so, how much? and how long can you stay?

If you were to lose stable housing,

- What shelters are in your area that you trust?

- Would you live in a motel temporarily? If so, determine which ones and find out what their weekly or monthly rates are.

- Would you try to keep your children with you or have them stay with family?

- Where would you keep your household goods?

Situation: Homelessness What to Do and What NOT to do

First Things First - Storage, Storage, Storage!!!

If you will be entering a situation where you have a lack or unstable housing, your first move must be to look for storage facilities with temperature controlled units for your household goods. This will be a monthly expense, but you must do it, as having your personal belongings in a secure environment during this transition will be vital for your recovery. Make sure the facility has gated entry and 24 hour surveillance. Look for a unit large enough to hold a 3 bedroom home worth of goods.

You will probably need to rent a truck unless you already have one. Be prepared to make multiple trips to get everything moved. I also recommend purchasing a small safe that can be kept there to contain your sensitive documents such as birth and marriage certificates, and social security cards.

Second, get a 6 or 12 month post office box from your local post office to receive mail and other small packages. The post office is a secure environment that is normally monitored with cameras. This will provide an alternative for you to receive personal mail without having to use the mailing address of friends, family, or whatever facility you are staying at.

Staying with Friends or Family

Do:

- Contribute towards monthly bills or take one bill to pay

- Keep your area clean and contribute to household maintenance such as washing dishes, cutting grass, doing laundry, vacuuming, etc.

Dont:

- Complain about anything
- Be lazy
- Come in late unless from work
- Overstay your welcome

Staying in a Motel

Do:

- Make sure the hotel area is safe and serves complimentary breakfast.

- Stock the fridge every 2 to 3 days with small items such as lunchmeat, milk, juice, items that don't need to be cooked.

- Take personal and valuable items with you when you leave your room.

- Take advantage of any opportunity to receive free meals or non-perishable food items, such as from a food bank.

- Maintain good personal hygiene and grooming habits. Make sure your clothes stay clean. Find out where the nearest laundromat is.

Don't:

- Tell strangers your personal information or share details regarding your housing situation.

- Spend a lot on food.

- Make it obvious you are homeless.

- Be afraid to use the motel address when applying for work or other assistance.

Staying in your car

Do:

- Research safest areas to park overnight for crime, drugs, lighting at night.
- Have a case of water, a cooler for ice and a thermal lunch bag.
- Have extra blankets and pillows.
- Look for area gyms, truck stops or gas stations with showers to maintain good hygiene. For gyms you will need to obtain a membership.
- Have an emergency first aid kit.

- Have a travel pack with personal hygiene items such as: toothbrush, toothpaste, baby wipes, soap, skin moisturizer, flushable wipes, deodorant, laundry detergent.

- Have a travel bag with other items such as: rain jacket, socks, underwear, cold jacket, dress shirts, dress pants, dress shoes, and a change of clothing.

- Have a food bag that has items such as: roll of paper towels, paper plates, plastic utensils, salt and pepper.

- Have any needed medication and acetaminophen or tylenol with you.

- Have washcloths and towels at least two of each.

Don't

- Stay in the same location every night unless you have permission from the property owner.

- Keep valuable items in your car.

- Make it obvious you are sleeping in your car and park close to lighting for safety.

- Spend a lot on food, make sure items are small enough to fit into a cooler.

- Fall asleep with the car running, ever!!

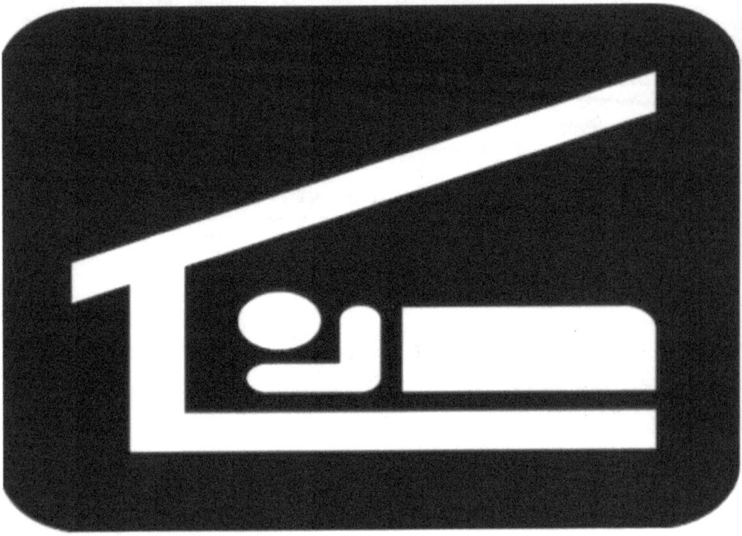

Staying in a Shelter

Do:

- Make sure the shelter is in a safe area and has security.
- Make sure there is an area to shower and perform other personal hygiene.
- Make sure they provide clean linen.
- Make sure you can use their address if needed.

Don't:

- Have valuable items or documents with you, try to find a friend or family member who can hold on to them, or keep them in a safe in your storage unit.. If that is not an option many banks have security boxes.

- Share personal information with strangers.

Do Persevere, Don't Give up on your Dreams..

You will climb your way out of situation D with hard work, discipline and perseverance. The goal isn't to jump back into plan A or B but to level up back to situation C. Take this opportunity to enhance your skills and talents. What can you do whether by natural skill or by training? Now may be the time to start working on establishing your own business.

Also, develop an exercise routine, something you can do without a gym membership or equipment. Maintaining good health and strength with diet and exercise is vitally important during these transitions and various situations.

A New Beginning...the Comeback

There are many avenues that lead not only towards getting back on your feet but finding success again, sometimes in unexpected areas. This section will discuss some of those avenues.

Reenlisting

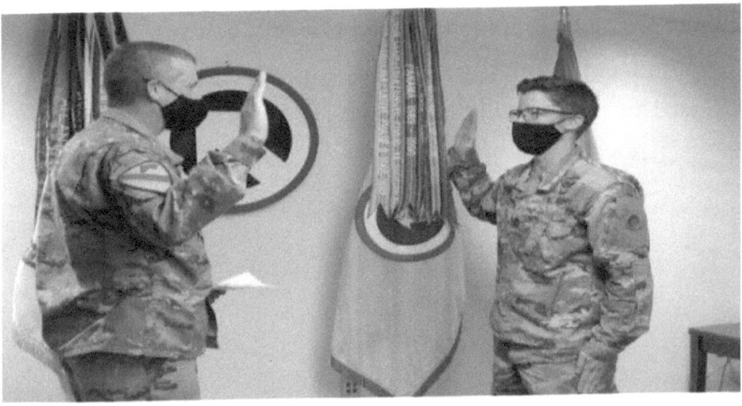

You may have noticed a running theme throughout this guide, that is maintaining the option of reenlistment. The reason, Life post military career is markedly different for a retiree, than for those who just end their service at the end of their enlistment contract.

For one, the access you have to housing, shopping, healthcare and other programs is on equal level with those on Active Duty. You get your own ID card which gives you access to any facility on base including fitness and recreation.

Even your spouse and children get a dependent ID card which gives them the same access. Your shopping privileges are unlimited, unlike those who don't retire who have to have a service connected disability.

Healthcare coverage options are greater for you and your immediate family. You may also be eligible to live on base, should that be an option you'd like to consider. In addition, your military pension holds at your pay grade upon retirement, which can in and of itself be enough to sustain your household.

On the other hand those that just let their time expire, such as I did, are reliant on the Veterans Administration for everything from healthcare to housing assistance. Neither of which is guaranteed. Your dependent's have no benefits. Your access to shopping, programs and facilities on military installations is limited, and once again only if you have a service connected disability.

My daughter who is now 17, spent the majority of her childhood on a military installation, she went to the daycare, and attended school on one. Now, her access is limited, unless she is with me, gets a visitors pass or works on base. Dependants of veterans, especially veterans who have been cleared to have base access should also have the same access to base resources.

Also, none of the years you spent in the service will be counted towards any retirement, unless you obtain a federal job that allows you to buy back, yes, I said buy, your service time back and have it count towards your new career time towards retirement. I have spoken with many Veterans who discharged at the end of their service contract, some with less than 5 years to retirement and even if they went on to have successful careers or businesses regret not staying to retirement if it was possible. We all agree you cut off a valuable resource that in the short or long run, would benefit not only you, but your family.

Hindsight is 20/20 but I am currently fighting to have legislation passed that would allow prior service members the ability to reenlist even if past 5 years since discharge without having to repeat basic training and allow those over 50 to reenlist if they have 12 years or less remaining to retirement. Considering the number of people over 50 currently serving, hopefully this age discrimination when it comes to military enlistment policy will soon end.

With new recruitment levels low and young people not inclined to join as in previous years, hopefully policy and regulation will soon change to allow older prior service members up to age 55 to reenlist. This age group is already trained, motivated and still has a lot to offer in service.

Should you decide reenlistment is a necessary option, make sure you speak with a recruiter that is familiar with the current reenlistment regulations for prior service members because they do change.

For example, I recently tried to reenlist back into the reserves, thinking I would just pick a MOS (military occupational specialty), and go to school for it. However, while I was going through the paperwork process I was told I would have to attend basic training again as the regulation had changed from 10 years out of service to 5 years without needing to repeat basic training. For some, that may be a pretty big deal.

You may also need to go back through MEPS, so your medical history will be intensely scrutinized. Get as much information as possible upfront regarding openings in your area as well as eligibility for reenlistment bonuses and any waivers you may need.

I recommend, if you decide to go this route, take the time to discuss with your family the level of commitment and sacrifice that will be required possibly for many years to come, especially if your aim, which it should be, is military retirement.

The Individual Ready Reserve (IRR)

I wanted to mention this option that may not be too well known in the military community. The IRR allows you to maintain your status as a service member but you are considered inactive. You are assigned to a reserve unit but you don't report for any duty except for a muster maybe once a year for accountability and to make sure your records are up to date.

The good thing about the IRR is, your retirement clock continues to tick, the only difference is, you won't have the retirement points, those servicemembers that drill do. However, these can be acquired by taking online classes.

If you have not yet discharged or have recently discharged, but you are not sure about continuing in the service, take a break and go into the IRR until you make a final decision. I did this, but came out of it and started to drill again, only to break my arm and let my time run out, when I should have stuck it out.

Pursuing a different career path

It may be necessary to look into another career field or profession from what you initially wanted to pursue upon discharge. Examine your skills and training to see in what areas you would excel as a career.

For example, if you have excellent customer service skills, you should consider healthcare, hospitality or other customer service career options. If you are someone good at giving detailed, easy to understand instructions, becoming a teacher, a profession highly in demand, is also another example of how using a natural skill can help expand your employment options.

You may find many more doors open including management positions highly attainable in a relatively short period of time.

It's not only thinking outside the box but actually taking yourself out of the box you put yourself in so you are ready for new opportunities.

Paid training programs

Consider training programs that offer some form of monthly, bi weekly or weekly training. You must maintain a steady stream of income to cover daily and monthly expenses. While you are in training take advantage of any free food that is offered. If time allows, do some additional side work such as delivery driving or anything else you may be skilled or gifted to do.

Some schools or organizations don't offer pay, but tuition costs are covered along with other fees if you meet certain stipulations such as you agree to work for the organization after program completion.

For example, some hospitals will cover nursing school tuition and fees for people interested in the nursing profession, if they agree to work for that hospital for 1 to 3 years after graduation. The same is true for some in demand professions, such as electricians, and teachers.

Entrepreneurship

For those of you with business ideas, whether it be to buy into an existing franchise or starting your own from scratch, this section is for you and can be put into planning no matter what situation or plan you are in.

Plan A, Plan B, Plan C or **Plan D** becoming an entrepreneur can start in any of these plans or situations, but it will require a lot of hard work, dedication and determination.

You may already have side businesses that you may be looking or ready to expand into a full time profession or career. Regardless of which category you are in, there is one critical step you must take that will give you the best foundation. Research.

Research, the following for either scenario for your business plan:

Product - Is there a demand? What are production and manufacturing requirements? Is it scalable?

Services - Is there a need? Will you need a staff?

Market - who is the customer/base or target market?

A market analysis will cover current and potential demand for your goods or service, along with existing competition. For example, when you have a business such as a bakery or barbershop, it is critical to emphasize what makes your specific business different from a similar business. In some cases it may be as simple as better hours of availability, or the ideal location.

Location - is potential location in a high pedestrian traffic area, high visibility area? This will be important if you have a brick and mortar business reliant on walk-in customers.

Startup Costs - what are the estimated startup costs? Include franchise buy in costs. There are many federal, and private grants and loans for small business startups, look into those for veterans and if applicable for minority owned businesses.

Profit Margin - after expenses, what is your estimated net profit margin?

Developing a **Cost/Risk Analysis** will help determine startup and ongoing monthly expenses, operating costs and equipment depreciation.

Taxes - make sure you research local, state and federal tax requirements for your business.

Becoming an entrepreneur or business owner is not quick or easy, even if it's doing something you have been doing your entire life. However, it can be the most rewarding as you are pursuing a career option not only that you enjoy, but also gives you personal fulfillment. With hard work, one day your business may be successful enough to be your primary income source and those changes in plans may have worked in your favor to push you to a better place.

Conclusion

Preparation for your separation from military service should begin as early as possible. Ideally, development of your **Plan A** should begin no less than 18 months before your discharge date. **Plan B** should be developed within 6 to 12 months of discharge date.

Plans C and **D** are where planning for the unexpected comes in. This book and the assignments contained therein, are designed to help guide you through those unplanned circumstances. For it's not the event, situation or circumstance, but how prepared you are, and your response, that will determine what happens next.

The key to planning for life after your DD214 is to be proactive prior to your discharge, during transition, and frequently thereafter.

We may not have all served in combat environments, but we all served in some capacity, and were trained to maintain situational awareness, adapt, and overcome. So, no matter what situation you are in or face, your service member to civilian transition operation can be a success.

Resources and other service agencies

Benefits and Support Organizations

Department of Veterans Affairs (VA.gov)

For Veterans Administration benefits including healthcare and education benefits. Many cities have local Vet centers that help with registration, obtaining an ID card and submitting paperwork for benefits.

MilitaryOneSource

For information regarding military, service members, and veteran news and policy updates across all branches.

Disabled Veterans of America (DAV.org)

Assisting veterans with having a better quality of life, including job fairs, activities, and rides to appointments. All services are free

American Legion, (legion.org)

Wartime veterans service organization that also assists veterans with employment services, records, other activities. Most American Legions can be found locally.

Wounded Warrior Project

Charity that assists wounded veterans with a variety of programs including, housing assistance, sports and other activities.

Careers

USAJOBS.gov - primary website for federal, government and some public service jobs. You can build a resume (recommended) and upload all relevant documents that will assist in obtaining hiring preferences. These are also good employment resources:

Recruitmilitary.com

Careeronestop.org

Fedshirevets.gov

There are also many social media groups that offer support and information for all veterans and currently serving servicemembers.

Also by Melody Young

Making America Great by Building it Better
Transitions Operation DD214 and Beyond

About the Author

Born and raised in Brooklyn, New York, Melody is a married, mother of three children.

She joined the Army like many others shortly after the September 11, 2001 attacks. She would serve with a medical instructor unit and then a combat engineer unit. After returning from her deployment to Afghanistan she decided to discharge to be home with her young daughter.

Currently, she is the owner of an event management company and a mobile food truck business based in Augusta, Georgia.

This guide is a compilation of some of the experiences she has had and the many lessons learned that she hopes will help others in their transition from servicemember to civilian.

www.ingramcontent.com/pod-product-compliance
Lightning Source LLC
LaVergne TN
LVHW090427210926
848480LV00002B/717
* 9 7 9 8 2 1 5 8 1 9 9 7 5 *